Paid for by donations

from the

Mount Laurel Community

LIFE STORIES

THOMAS JEFFERSON

Gillian Gosman

PowerKiDS press.
New York

Published in 2011 by The Rosen Publishing Group, Inc.
29 East 21st Street, New York, NY 10010

First Edition

Editor: Jennifer Way
Book Design: Ashley Burrell and Erica Clendening

Photo Credits: Cover (inset), pp. 4–5, 6–7, 10–11 SuperStock/Getty Images; cover (background), pp. 13, 19 Hulton Archive/Getty Images; pp. 6, 15, 16–17 MPI/Getty Images; pp. 8–9 Studio of Sir William Beechey/The Bridgeman Art Library/Getty Images; p. 10 www.iStockphoto.com/Chris Pecoraro; pp. 12, 22 (top) Fotosearch/Getty Images; p. 14 Joseph Sohm-Visions of America/Getty Images; pp. 17, 20–21, 22 (bottom) Stock Montage/Getty Images; p. 18 Wikipedia Commons.

Library of Congress Cataloging-in-Publication Data

Gosman, Gillian.
 Thomas Jefferson / by Gillian Gosman. — 1st ed.
     p. cm. — (Life stories)
 Includes index.
 ISBN 978-1-4488-3178-4 (library binding) — ISBN 978-1-4488-3180-7 (pbk.) —
ISBN 978-1-4488-3181-4 (6-pack)
 1. Jefferson, Thomas, 1743-1826—Juvenile literature. 2. Presidents—United States—Biography—Juvenile literature. 3. United States—Politics and government—1775-1783—Juvenile literature.
 4. United States—Politics and government—1783-1865—Juvenile literature. I. Title.
 E332.79.G67 2011
 973.4'6092—dc22
 [B]

                                    2010037803

Manufactured in the United States of America
CPSIA Compliance Information: Batch #WW11PK: For Further Information contact Rosen Publishing, New York, New York at 1-800-237-9932

Contents

Meet Thomas Jefferson 4

Young Thomas 6

Life in Colonial America 8

At Home and at War 10

The Declaration of Independence 12

Virginia and Beyond 14

Vice President Jefferson 16

President Jefferson 18

Jefferson's Last Years 20

Timeline 22

Glossary 23

Index 24

Web Sites 24

Meet Thomas Jefferson

Thomas Jefferson was the third president of the United States. He is also the person who wrote the Declaration of Independence.

There were many sides to Jefferson. He wrote about

Thomas Jefferson was a student, an inventor, an architect, a writer, and a statesman.

the value of freedom. At the same time, though, he was a slave owner. Learning about the different sides of Jefferson's life is an important part of understanding the history of early America.

YOUNG THOMAS

Thomas Jefferson was born on April 13, 1743. He grew up on Shadwell, his family's **plantation** in Virginia. Thomas Jefferson's father died when Thomas was 14 years old. He left Thomas his land and his slaves.

The slaves in this picture are working on a tobacco plantation. Tobacco was an important crop in Colonial Virginia.

Schools and learning were important to Jefferson. He founded the University of Virginia in 1819.

Jefferson had a lifelong love of learning. He went to the College of William and Mary at age 16. People said he studied for 15 hours every day!

Life in Colonial America

Thomas Jefferson was born when Virginia was one of the North American **colonies** ruled by Great Britain. The king of Britain ruled the colonists.

Jefferson believed that it was unfair that the colonists did not have

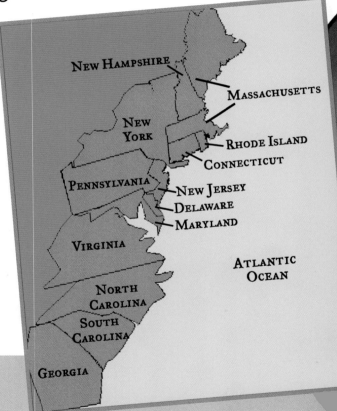

NEW HAMPSHIRE

MASSACHUSETTS

NEW YORK

RHODE ISLAND

CONNECTICUT

PENNSYLVANIA

NEW JERSEY

DELAWARE

MARYLAND

VIRGINIA

ATLANTIC OCEAN

NORTH CAROLINA

SOUTH CAROLINA

GEORGIA

This map shows the 13 colonies of North America as they were in the mid-1700s.

King George III, shown here, was king of Great Britain from 1760 until 1820.

representatives to speak for them in the British government. By the 1760s and the 1770s, many colonists spoke about wanting to break away from British rule.

At Home and at War

In 1768, Jefferson began building Monticello. This is his plantation in Virginia.

In 1769, Jefferson joined the Virginia House of Burgesses. This was the Virginia Colony's government.

This is Monticello, Jefferson's plantation in Virginia. ↑

When Jefferson joined the Second Continental Congress, in 1775, the group's main job was to plan the Colonial war effort.

In 1775, the colonies began fighting the **American Revolution** to win **independence** from Britain. That year, Jefferson was asked to be a representative in the Second Continental Congress.

The Declaration of Independence

In 1776, the Continental Congress asked Jefferson to put in writing the Congress's reasons for voting for independence from Great Britain.

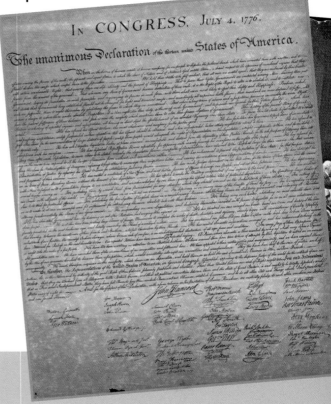

This is a signed copy of the Declaration of Independence.

This painting shows Jefferson (center) presenting the Declaration of Independence to the Second Continental Congress.

Jefferson's document was called the Declaration of Independence. The Congress approved the declaration on July 4, 1776. The 13 colonies had now formed a new, independent nation.

Virginia and Beyond

In 1776, Jefferson was elected to Virginia's House of Delegates, the state's **legislature**. In 1779, he became Virginia's **governor**.

Here is Virginia's capitol building in Richmond. As Virginia's governor, Jefferson pushed for freedom of religion.

Here is Secretary of State Jefferson (second from left) with other members of George Washington's cabinet.

In 1783, Jefferson was picked to be a member of the U.S. Congress. In 1785, he became the U.S. representative to France. In 1790, President George Washington picked Jefferson to be his secretary of state.

Vice President Jefferson

In the nation's early years, presidential **candidates** did not run for office with a vice presidential candidate. Instead, the candidate with the most votes in the **Electoral College** became president.

Vice President Jefferson and President Adams belonged to different political parties. They did not agree on many things!

This is John Adams, second president of the United States.

The candidate with the second-highest number of votes became vice president. In 1796, Jefferson ran for president. He came in second and became John Adams's vice president.

President Jefferson

In 1800, Jefferson ran for president again. This time, the election ended in a tie between Jefferson and Aaron Burr.

The House of Representatives had to pick the winner. They voted 36 times before

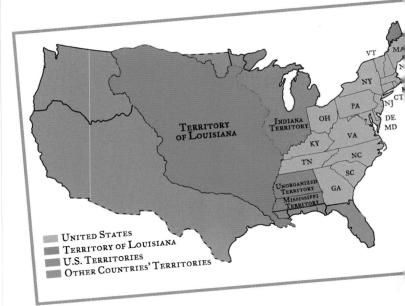

When Jefferson bought the territory of Louisiana (green) from France, he doubled the size of the United States.

Aaron Burr was Jefferson's vice president during his first term. George Clinton was vice president during Jefferson's second term.

agreeing that Jefferson would be president and Burr vice president. During Jefferson's presidency, the United States bought the **territory** of Louisiana from France in 1803.

Jefferson's Last Years

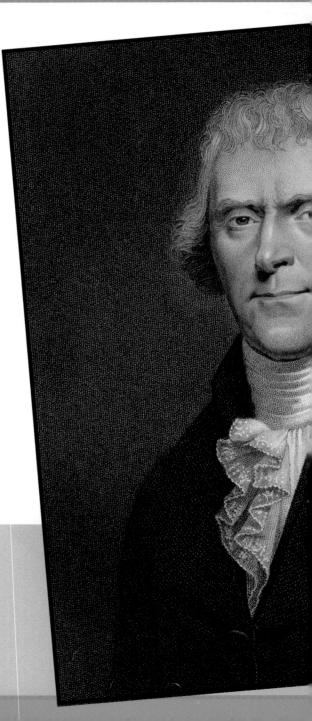

Jefferson was reelected president in 1804. His time in the office had highs and lows. He made it illegal to bring slaves into the country. He also started the forced removal of Native Americans from the South.

Jefferson died on July 4, 1826. This date was the fiftieth anniversary of the approval of the Declaration of Independence.

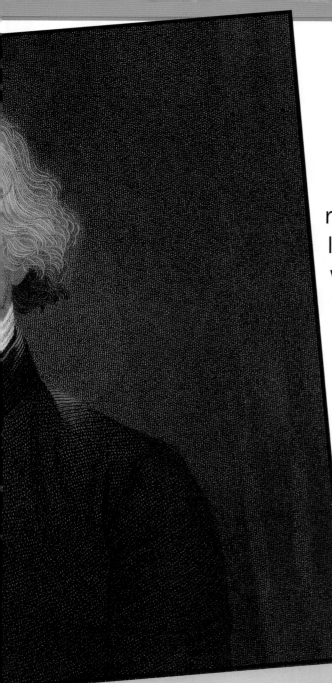

In 1809, Jefferson returned to Monticello to a life of farming, inventing, and writing. On July 4, 1826, Thomas Jefferson died at the age of 83.

TIMELINE

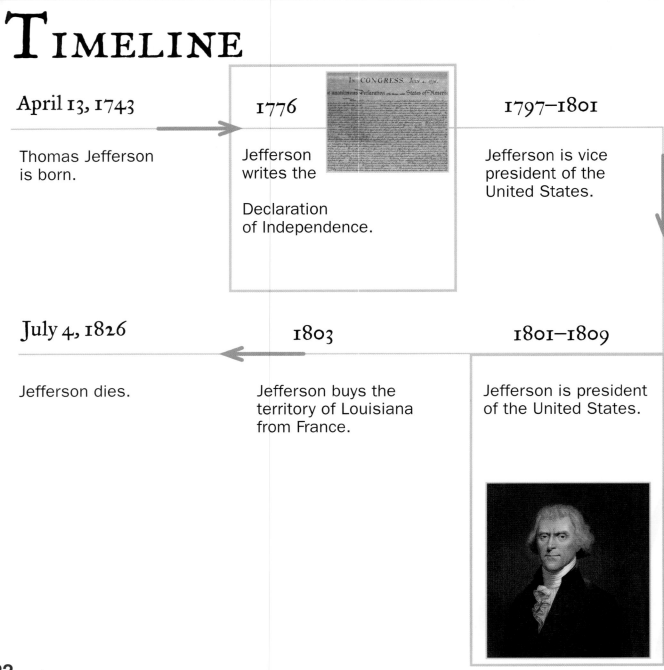

April 13, 1743

Thomas Jefferson is born.

1776

Jefferson writes the

Declaration of Independence.

1797–1801

Jefferson is vice president of the United States.

July 4, 1826

Jefferson dies.

1803

Jefferson buys the territory of Louisiana from France.

1801–1809

Jefferson is president of the United States.

Glossary

American Revolution (uh-MER-uh-ken reh-vuh-LOO-shun) Battles that soldiers from the colonies fought against Britain for freedom, from 1775 to 1783.

candidates (KAN-dih-dayts) People who run in elections.

colonies (KAH-luh-neez) New places where people move that are still ruled by the leaders of the country from which they came.

Electoral College (ih-LEK-tuh-rul KO-lij) A group of people who pick the president based on who gets the most votes in their states.

governor (GUH-vun-ur) Someone elected as head of a state.

independence (in-dih-PEN-dents) Freedom from the control of other people.

legislature (LEH-jis-lay-chur) A body of people that has the power to make or pass laws.

plantation (plan-TAY-shun) A very large farm where crops are grown.

representatives (reh-prih-ZEN-tuh-tivz) People picked to speak for others.

territory (TER-uh-tor-ee) Land that is controlled by a person or a group of people.

Index

A

America, 5
American Revolution, 11

C

colonies, 8, 11, 13

E

Electoral College,
16

F

France, 15, 19, 22
freedom, 4

G

governor, 14

H

history, 5

I

independence,
11–12

L

legislature, 14

M

Monticello, 10, 21

P

plantation, 6, 10

R

representative(s),
9, 11, 15, 18

S

Shadwell, 6
slave owner, 5

V

value, 4
Virginia, 6, 8, 10

Web Sites

Due to the changing nature of Internet links, PowerKids Press has developed an online list of Web sites related to the subject of this book. This site is updated regularly. Please use this link to access the list:
www.powerkidslinks.com/life/tjeff/